Audition Monologues: Power Pieces for Women

A collection of dramatic and comedic one-minute monologues designed for ages 18 to 80.

By Deborah Maddox

A must have for amateur and professional actors alike.

Website: www.auditionmonologues.com

Audition Monologues: Power Pieces for Women
Copyright 2003/Deborah Maddox
All rights reserved

ISBN # 0-9716827-1-2

Published by:
Lucid Solutions
P.O. Box 32141
Mesa, Arizona 85275-2141

www.auditionmonologues.com

*A **woman:*** *Intriguing, loving, deeply complicated, dedicated, self-indulging, strong, anxious, honest, successful, manipulative, paranoid, driven, witty, intoxicated, sexual, nurturing, lazy, peaceful, supportive, deceitful, inspiring, fearful, giving, uniquely beautiful, humorous...and yet she has many faces.*

You will find her in this book...

This book is dedicated to all women of my life, past and present...and I thank you.

Book Description...

This book has it all! Audition Tested, Industry Approved!
Audition Monologues: Power Pieces for Women is a collection of dramatic and comedic monologues designed for
women between the ages of 18 and 80. Expressively written in a way to enable the actor to project emotional range
effectively and to experience the situation of the character,
first hand. The content is powerful, includes surprising
twists, and is appealing to both professional and amateur
actors. Industry professionals such as casting directors,
agents, acting coaches and actors have highly praised this
book and actively recommend it to their colleagues and
peers. Often casting decisions are made within one-
minute's time, therefore, a two to four minute monologue
can be lengthy and inappropriate. Audition Monologues:
Power Pieces for Women offers over 60 monologues with
unlimited character choices. Also includes valuable audition tips written from an Agent's point of view.

Table of Contents

Drama Continued...

Comedy

How To Pick The Right Material

The material an actor chooses for the audition is essential. This choice can make or break the outcome of an audition. Considering the fact that the audition process tends to be lengthy, a two to four minute monologue can be too long and inappropriate. *In fact, casting decisions are often made within one minute's time.* Most often, the determination of whether or not the actor possesses strong acting skills is made within the first thirty seconds of delivery. During the next thirty seconds, the decision is made whether or not to add the actor to the callback list.

Give the industry professionals what they want to see: *a one-minute power piece.* **Audition Monologues: Power Pieces for Women** provides *strong audition quality material,* which enables the actor to be creative with her own character development and versatility. This book contains a variety of dramatic and comedic monologues for women. When performed, the monologues are delivered from a first person point of view, enabling the actor to project emotional range and to experience the situation of the character, first hand. These monologues are powerful because they are based on real-life experiences. They are written in a style that allows the actor to readily identify with the character and play out the scenario effectively.

Acting is a wonderful way to express creativity and talent. Remember that there are no two people on this earth who are the same. Therefore, when you audition, give of yourself. Find confidence in knowing that your delivery is unique. If you have the passion within yourself to perform, it will be recognized and, eventually, be appreciated by others.

I hope you enjoy performing these monologues as much as I have enjoyed writing them. Relax, focus and bring it all together. May you keep them on the edge of their seats.

Happy Auditioning!

How To Prepare For An Audition

For amateur and experienced actors alike, the *audition* is a significant part of acting. Although the nature of each audition may be different, the etiquette consistently remains the same. Whether the audition is for a role in film, television, theater or simply for agency representation, the audition is a systematic process in which industry professionals make final casting decisions. Industry professionals may consist of casting directors, producers, directors or agency representatives.

The Audition: Excitement, anticipation, anxiety, confidence. These are just a few emotions an actor may experience during an audition because final decisions are made through this process. Along with strong acting skills, it is imperative to possess strong auditioning skills. How you present yourself and the impression that is made will greatly affect the outcome of the audition.

The following are four valuable guidelines that every actor should consider for an audition.

Marketability – Being seen as suitable for a part ultimately lies in the hands of the industry professionals. However, there are ways of beating the odds. For example, producers, directors and writers always have an idea of what they are looking for. Have you heard the phrase, "I'll know it when I see it?" The purpose of the audition is for the industry professionals to find the actor that they have visualized for the part. Before you go to an audition, be clear on what they are seeking. Often you will be informed of appropriate wardrobe for the part. If wardrobe requirements have not been stated, then dress simple, wearing colors that bring out your eyes and work best with your hair color. Wear little or no jewelry. You want the focus to be on you and your delivery, not your shiny bracelet or trendy outfit. Be prepared to be flexible, and if given the chance, show that you can portray a variety character types and emotional range.

Professionalism – Professionalism is the foundation of strong audition etiquette. The entertainment industry is a business, just like any other profession. It should never be looked at as a playground for egos. During the audition process, industry professionals are not only looking for acting ability. They are also anticipating a long-term relationship for the duration of time it will take to complete their project. They consider whether or not the actor's will be easy to work with and that they can take direction well.

When you enter an audition room, enter with confidence and a smile. Introduce yourself and shake hands with each person in the room. If you are asked any questions or if you are asked to tell a little about yourself, offer full and complete sentences. Yes and no answers are rarely effective. Refrain from putting the interviewers on a pedestal. Remember that they are people, just like you. If you find your nerves starting to escalate, you may want to try to visualize everyone in the room in their pajamas. That may help you to see things on the lighter side.

Take advantage of the audition time to be yourself. Leave an effective and memorable impression without over-extending your welcome. Listen to direction, take your mark and give it your best shot. If you make a mistake, continue on. They are not looking for perfection, just a strong delivery and effective characterization. Never ask to start over. If they want to see you do it again, they will make that request. If you are performing a monologue, only state the name of the piece. Generally they are not interested in the full story line, and time is of importance. When *slating* your name, take advantage of those few seconds to let your personality shine. Remember, you can tell a lot about a person just by their "hello."

Characterization – Whether you are performing a monologue, dialogue or commercial script, getting into character is key. Give great thought to the character's persona. Visualize the character in your mind and decide if the character is soft spoken or condescending. Maybe she is strong-willed, over-confident or insecure. Perhaps the character has a nervous twitch. Decide what kind of personality you will give the character. What about the demeanor? Be deliberate with the body language you choose for the character. One of the greatest things about being an actor is that what you offer is completely up to you. Regardless of the specifics you choose to implement, be creative and find confidence in your choices.

Reaction – When you perform a monologue at an audition, there are no props or acting partners available to respond to. Therefore, it is up to you to create and visualize the stage and circumstances within your own mind, then effectively perform it so that the industry professionals visualize the same thing you are projecting. Take a moment and think about the art of pantomime. The mime communicates everything through facial expression and body language. Generally, it is not effective for actors to pretend to pick up a phone or take a sip of tea from an invisible teacup. However, like the mime, it is very effective for actors to communicate through facial expression and body language.

Many actors forget this factor while performing monologues. They tend to get so involved with their own delivery and how they are going to say the words, that they dismiss the relationship with their acting partner or prop, invisible or otherwise. Think and feel during the delivery of each line. Demonstrating that particular skill will greatly enhance any performance.

When you perform a monologue, you must paint a mental picture for the audience, a clear picture of the circumstances relating to each situation. Deliver your reaction and projection effectively, and you will have them at the edge of their seats.

Focus on the character and have fun with it. Remember, there is no right way, just your way.

Enjoy!

Drama

The Perfectionist
Drama
18+

When it comes to this relationship, nothing is ever good enough.

Yes. OK? I admit it. I make mistakes. So does everyone else. I'm not perfect. I will never be perfect, no matter how hard I try. You expect so much from me. I feel like when I do screw up, my whole world is going to crumble because you are sure to remind me of how much of a failure you think I am. Sometimes I just want to end it all. Yeah, that's right. Just stop living. Did you know that when I go to the grocery store, I spend twenty minutes trying to pick the perfect tomatoes for you? I spend twenty minutes on your stupid tomatoes! Perfection! That's what it's all about, isn't it? Well, I give up. I'm not perfect and I could spend hours looking for the best tomatoes. But I will never find them, will I? Will I? No matter what I do, no matter how hard I try, in your eyes, it will never be enough…never.

Notes:_____

_____

Seconds Thoughts
Drama
30+

She speaks to a colleague about how she is feeling about her patients. It all is becoming very overwhelming.

I just can't seem to handle it the way I used to. I was always able to put it somewhere...you know...remind myself that I am the professional and that it is my job to convey information, not emotion. But, now? On more days than some I am telling people...that there is nothing that I can do. Everything is getting to me. Everyday I see the pain they go through. I watch as the families come to visit, trying to keep their spirits up. This morning, I learned that Mr. Lawrence in room 304 has a 5-year-old daughter. Tomorrow, I am the one who will discuss his test results with him. I have to tell him that he has, maybe, six months to live. My patients have families, husbands, wives, children, friends, people who love them. I feel like I am the one who is cutting their lives too short. When I decided to practice medicine, I thought I would be saving lives. Yet, lately, I am the constant messenger of bad news. You know, it's crazy when you think about it. Life is so wonderful. Why does death have to be so painful? It just doesn't seem fair.

Notes:_____

_____

Paranoid
Drama
18+

Although she is under full supervision of a psychiatric doctor, she still feels scared and alone. There seems no way out of the madness. She begs for the doctor to understand and save her from her terror.

You have to be smart and look around the corners! Always look around the corners. And don't forget to check underneath the bed. Why? Because...they always hide in those places. And their voices. Oh God...all of those voices, crying out. Can't you hear them? Listen! Listen to them! Sleep? I don't want to sleep! If I sleep, they will get me. Why can't you understand that? I keep telling you. If I sleep, they will get me. Please don't let them get me. Just tell them to shut-up and go away. I can't take it anymore! The voices...the screaming...the yelling....They are so loud. And the laughing. Why are they laughing? Please help me. Just make them go away. No...don't leave me alone in this room another night! No! Don't go! I'll be good. I promise. Please, Doctor, I promise to be good. Don't let them get me! No, don't leave!

Notes:_____

_____

When Can I Live Again?
Drama
20+

After tragically losing a special friend, she wonders when it will be OK to live again.

Today, all I know is what it feels like to live life without you. Yet, yesterday, my life was full...because of you. You were there to make me laugh...to listen to my thoughts...you were there as my friend. Today the sun shines...and I only wish for the sun to refuse to shine. I don't want a new day to begin. It just doesn't seem right. How can I wake up to the light, knowing you are gone...forever. I want to keep my eyes closed, because I can't see how I can open them knowing that you are not here anymore. Last night seems so close...like a second ago...you were just here. If I think real hard, for a moment, maybe I can remember how I used to be...before you...but then what? When will it be OK for the sun to shine again?

Notes:_____

_____

Erase Hate
Drama
18+

She decides to confront someone whom embodies ignorance.

So here you stand, right in front of me, judging me. Who are you to judge me? Of course we have differences, but that shouldn't be a bad thing. Don't you realize that there are no two people on this earth who are exactly the same? Nobody is the same. Why can't you appreciate our differences and see how we are alike? But you choose to close your eyes. Well, open them! You are a person. I am a person. We both go to work everyday. We both have friends. We both have families. Whether you want to admit it or not, we both have feelings. We are two people trying to figure out how to live in this world. Look, I haven't figured it all out, but I do know who I am and what I believe. And there you stand, right in front of me, unable to look past the color of my skin.

Notes:_____

_____

Change
Drama
20+

She knew he was having an affair, but she had no idea the extent of it. She is concerned about how their son will adjust to the change.

What about Kenny? I am curious to know, during the moment, right before you decided to drop this bomb on me, did you ever think of how your decision was going to effect your son? He is a little boy who is in love with his daddy. How are you going to explain this to him? He will never understand. He is smart, Tony, and eventually he will start asking me questions. What am I going to say? Maybe something like, "I'm sorry Kenny, but Daddy has fallen in love with someone else." Then maybe I should go a little further and tell him the whole truth, because I think it will be a little confusing for him when he goes to visit you on weekends and he sees you go into the same bedroom with his so called, "Uncle" Marty. I thought that you were having an affair, but...with a man? Look, I know that there is no turning back, but I also know that Kenny will be in your life forever. I am just not so sure how he is going to deal with something like this, especially when he gets older. What are we going to say?

Notes:_____

_____

_____

One More Chance
Drama
20+

Love walked in the room, yet she regretfully declined a chance for happiness.

He has chosen someone else to be with, someone else to have children with, someone else to spend his life with. Every time our eyes met, I saw myself with him. I wanted him so much...but I just couldn't. Yet, I saw him by my side. I saw him in my life. I saw him...with me. He wanted me and he was persistent. Unfortunately, I was as persistent as he was... because my persistence was to close all doors. This sweet, smart, sexy, beautiful man... pursued me...me. And I what did I do? I closed every door. Now look at me, feeling sorry for myself. When I look into the mirror, I can't even give myself sympathy, because I know that I don't deserve it. I made a choice, a conscious choice...based on fear. FEAR! Now, it's too late. He has moved on. And really, I can't say that I blame him, but a part of me was hoping that he would wait for me...wait for me to get off this crazy ride of fear. I guess life just doesn't work that way, does it?

Notes:_____

_____

I Know Now
Drama
18+

She finally releases the guilt regarding the loss of her boy-friend.

Everything that I have left of you is behind this closet door. I don't dare get within two feet of it, for if I open it, I open the memory of you and all of the pain that comes with that memory. I can't do that anymore. It hurts too much. I have to move on now...without the pain. I know now that if I am to continue to live my life, I must say goodbye, friend, for if I hang on to you, I will die inside. If I had one more chance to sit face to face with you, I would say that I am sorry for not getting to you soon enough. If I had, maybe things would be different. I don't mean different for us, but I mean different for you. I am sorry for not believing you when you told me you wanted to die, for I know now, you were crying for help. How was I supposed to know? Finally, I wish that I could have breathed enough air into your lungs to give you your life back, but I know now...that I am not a source of life. I know now, I am just a student.

Notes:_____

_____

_____

Loneliness
Drama
20+

Too much time has passed and she finds herself tolerating an unhealthy marriage. Finally, she sees the light.

I come home to a husband every night and yet, I am the loneliest person on earth. How is it when we have conversation, there is none. Then comes the moment of silence, where there is nothing more to say. Even the joke that I heard earlier in the day isn't good enough. Eventually I remove myself from the room…shaking my head and asking myself, why? Why do I stay? I am married to someone who is completely incapable of seeing me for who and what I am. All he can see is a cook, a mother and a maid. I am so much more than that. He has no idea that I touch hearts...that I make a difference in this world, everyday. He can't imagine that. But the sad part is, deep down, he feels he is worthy of only one kind of woman… the kind of woman who is only capable of serving him. That's why he can't see me.

Notes:_____

_____

The Alcoholic Sister
Drama
18+

After becoming extremely obnoxious, her sister makes her leave the party.

Doesn't anyone know how to have fun around here? Come on! Loosen up, will ya? What's wrong with a little dancing? Who wants to dance with me? Come on, feel the music. What a bunch of party poopers. Don't you know how to have a good time? Get with it, people! Let's have some fun. What? Embarrassing you? I'm not embarrassing you, Sis. I am just having a good time. Will you stop it? I am fine. It is so like you to try to mess up a good time…and it's always my good time. Don't touch me. Stop. Just stop it. I am just trying to have some fun. But, like always, here you are accusing me of having too much to drink. Would you lay off for once? When did it become a crime to have fun? I just want to get everyone in the mood to dance a little. What's wrong with that? I am not drunk! Stop it! Don't touch me. OK, fine. I will go somewhere else and party. Yeah, that's a lot better than being with you and your lame friends. Hey Sis, don't call me. I'll call you. You're all boring anyway. I'll go have fun somewhere else…a place I won't get ragged on…Sis…good ole…Sis.

Notes:_____

_____

_____

Final Words
Drama
18+

Letting go of someone you love is never easy, unless they are worth letting go.

I know it's late. I'm sorry. Did I get you out of bed? I know you said not to come over here, but I just needed to see you again. I miss not having you around. I miss waking up with you. Please, let me finish. I know we fight a lot and that's why you left, but I still love you. The cat is even depressed. Please, can I come in? Can we just talk about it? Wh...who, who is that? I can't believe this. It's been only three weeks since you left! Three weeks and you are already screwing somebody else? You bastard! I guess the time we had together means nothing, huh? Is that it? Tell me, did you break up with me so you could be with her? I can't believe this. I thought I would come over here to show some effort...to compromise a little...to save something that I thought was worth saving. Well, I guess I thought wrong.

Notes:_____

_____

_____

The Unwarranted Affair
Drama
20+

She has just admitted to having an affair with her college roommate's father.

Wait! just wait! Stop yelling at me and let me explain. Yes, I know. I know he's your father. Just listen to me for a minute. It started at your graduation party. I was dancing by myself and he came up next to me. What was I supposed to do? He started dancing with me. In my mind, I thought because he was your dad, I should be nice to him. Lindsey, wait. Don't leave. Please let me try to explain. After we danced, we sat down and just talked... and laughed. We had so much in common with each other. I just went with it. I know that's hard for you to believe, but it's true. We like the same movies, the same art, the same...everything. At that point, I forgot who he was. At that point, he became interesting, someone I'd like to get to know. You can't fault me for that. You would have done the same thing. Look, I'm sorry. Believe me, if the tables were turned and it were you and my own father, I would feel the same way. Please don't hate me. I don't want to lose you as a friend. And, I don't want to lose him, either. Lindsey, please, try to understand.

Notes:_____

_____

Money Isn't Everything
Drama
18+

She decides to choose love over money. She confronts her pretentious mother with pride.

I don't care about the money! Don't you realize, I've never cared about the money, Mother? I never learned to appreciate it, anyway. How could I? All of my life, I have been raised by nannies and servants. Wow! What a life! You are just going to have to accept it. I love him... very much, and he has asked me to marry him. These days, Mother, there are no pre-arranged marriages. I am free to marry whomever I want. Do you actually think that happiness for me is having tea with some pretentious mother-in-law who will always judge what I am wearing and try to remember how many times I've worn it? Mark makes me laugh. He cares. He actually cares about what I say. When was the last time you and Daddy laughed together? Yes, I realize what I am walking away from. Money. Big deal! For me, that's easy. What I can't understand is why it is so easy for you to turn your back on my happiness? Is money and status that important to you?

Notes:_____

_____

A Long Time Comin
Drama
25+

*In a small rural town, this company pep talk is the last
one she will ever attend. She finally speaks up for herself
and the other hardworking employees.*

Excuse me, Sir? May I say somethin'? I have been sittin'
here listenin' to you talk about how this company has
grown over the past seven years and how yur profits have
gone up. You really caught my attention when you mentioned how hard work pays off. Why don't you put yur
money where yur mouth is, Sir? I have been here for all
of those seven years. Hard work pays off? Sir, can you
tell me how that statement affects me, or Franklin Brown,
or MaryLee Webster over there? How about all of us employees in this room, for that matter? I am still driving the
same car as I did when you hired me. I've seen yur brand
new Mercedes. Where are those raises you keep pro-
misin'?" Today, you talked about how someday our hard
work with pay off. With all due respect, Sir, it looks like
yur the only one who's benefitin'. I'm a single mother. I
have a baby to take care of and frankly, I can't afford to
work for someone like you. I gave ya seven years of my
life and I am finally realizin'...you're just full of a bunch
of hot air. I quit.

Notes:_____

_____

Memories
Drama
60+

She escapes the present moment and fondly remembers her life with her husband.

Ernest and I have been married for forty years. We never believed in divorce. Too messy. When you say those wedding vows, they mean forever. These days, young people don't understand that. Sure we have had our problems. And over the years I've picked up my share of his dirty socks and underwear up off the floor. When I think about it, I have made dinner after dinner for that man. I've ironed more shirts than I care to remember... and...yet, he has given me some of the most beautiful flowers I have ever seen. At times, he has made me laugh so hard I thought I would just burst. We have traveled the world and done so much together. When you look at our children, you know it was right. Our forty years have been so full...Oh, I'm sorry young man. I guess I got a little off track. Yes, I want Ernest to be cremated. That was his wish.

Notes:_____
_____
_____

Spare Change?
Drama
20+

Being homeless doesn't necessarily mean you're a junky. Sometimes, it is as simple as being a victim of unfortunate circumstances.

Excuse me, Maam? Can you spare some change? Bitch. Look at her. All dressed up, actin' like she has a purpose. Probably a dinner date or somethin'. Well, you know what? I have a purpose too! Three of 'em. Boys. I couldn't make ends meet, so here I am. That lady who just walked away, she looks at me like everybody else does. I've been told everything like "Go and get a job, Dummy" or "Quit livin' off the system." I never thought it could happen to me, being homeless and all. My husband worked at the factory. I stayed home with the kids. We never had no extra money, but we got by. I had never done any work before. Got married at fifteen. When he died, he left us with nothin'. Nobody would hire me with no experience and all. So here I am, askin' for help. The shelter don't give us no money, just a place to sleep. Yesterday, this one lady came right up to my face and yelled, "Maybe you should get off the drugs." But I don't do drugs. You got that? I don't do drugs! Just tryin' to survive, that's all.

Notes:_____

_____

Courage and Strength
Drama
25+
Under unbelievable circumstances, strength prevails.

Strong? I am not the strong one here. When they bring her back into the room from the treatments, she squeezes my hand and tells me how much it hurts, with no tears. That's when I give her a big hug and I tell her that everything is going to be OK. Of course, I don't know if it is going to be OK...or if it isn't. I'm dying inside. I try to be strong for her, but inside, this is killing me. The other day she looked up at me and asked why she couldn't just have a cold like other kids. Tell me, how do you explain to your child that you don't have the answer to that question? Why can't I look at my baby and tell her that she is going to get better? I ask God everyday, "Why? Why my baby?" Don't get me wrong, I would never wish this upon anyone...but...strong? I am not the strong one here. That's my daughter. She's the one who faces each day with courage and strength.

Notes:_____

_____

_____

Dignity
Drama
30+

She reacts to her socialite friends at the country club as they give their thoughts on how she should respond to the fact that her husband has had an affair.

Can you tell me why the wife is the last one to know? Seems like friends and business associates know more about your own marriage than you do. My husband informed me that he is not just having an affair, but that he has fallen in love with someone else. It's much more serious than just a little affair. Can it get any worse? I was truly in love with him…once…until yesterday. Damn him! I have raised our children. I committed myself 100% to that man. Tell me, Ladies, what happens to your husband for him to actually cross that line? Is that what a mid-life crisis is? And then for him to take it a step further, "I've fallen in love." Try infatuation. What a jerk! So now, how am I supposed to handle that kind of information? With dignity? How?

Notes:_____

_____

_____

Discrimination
Drama
30's +

Putting your heart and soul into your career doesn't always mean appreciation and reward from the bosses. As she realizes her reality, she hits it head on with confidence and strength.

Hold on Jim. As you know, I have been with this firm for six long years. I have seen more college graduate green peas come and go that I have lost track. If it weren't for me, you wouldn't have the O'Leary account. Admit it! That is one of your most lucrative accounts. This is the thanks I get? How many more years do I have to wait for an invitation for partnership? I am truly shocked. Well, it's got to be something. What is it? Not enough long days? Are my skirts too long? That's it, isn't it? I'm a woman! You're afraid to bring me in as partner because I'm a woman. Sure, it makes sense. This company has never had a female partner before. Admit it Jim, I threaten you because I am capable and because I am a woman. Well, you have only seen a small portion of the true strength of a woman. You think you feel threatened now. Today, you just declared war, Mister.

Notes:_____

_____

Before It's Too Late
Drama
20's +

When there is a beginning, there usually is an ending. She fears that her relationship with her longstanding boyfriend may end. But, her patience has run out. She finally tells him what's on her mind.

It's not like I am asking you to marry me. I'm not ready for that either. We are still young. There's no rush. All I'm saying is that I want to live with you. We practically live together anyway. Either I stay at your house or you end up staying at mine. Why pay two separate rent payments? Look, I have been thinking about this for awhile now. I've been very patient and I've given you your space. But, come on. After three years of being together, our relationship just isn't going anywhere. I love you so much. I am ready to take that next step. Come on, let's do it! Come on. Why? Why! I don't understand what you are so afraid of. OK, fine. But I'll tell you what I am afraid of. If we don't make some kind of change, our relationship will die. Please don't let that happen to us.

Notes:_____

_____

_____

Custody Battle
Drama
25+

Now, the inevitable is becoming reality. Her ex-husband is fighting for full custody of their young son. She begins to put things into perspective.

Sorry, I'm late. This day has been pure hell. Steve served me with custody papers. He is actually going to fight me for full custody of Andy. I can't believe it. You know what? Now that I think about it, I should have seen this coming. About six months ago, Andy told me that Vicki mentioned to him that he could call her "Mommy." She said that they were a family. I didn't say anything because I didn't want to start a fight. I've really tried to keep things smooth, you know? Andy told her he didn't want to call her Mommy anyway, and that I was his only Mommy. So I let it go. This is starting to make sense to me now. Last year, Steve and Vicki were trying to get pregnant. They tried everything, including intravenous fertilization. It didn't take. Well, it's so obvious, isn't it? They can't have kids of their own, so they are going for the next best thing. Mine. I may be a single mother, but they will get Andy over my dead body.

Notes:_____

_____

He's Back
Drama
18+

Her ex-boyfriend has come over to talk. Because it was so hard to get over him, she reluctantly lets him in. Since their breakup, she has gone through a great deal of personal growth.

What are you thinking? That you can pop right back into my life again? Pick up where we left off? You must think that I should just drop everything. Listen, I have a life now. No, I'm not serious with anyone yet. But that doesn't matter. Look, it has taken me a long time to get over you. You hurt me. A lot. This is amazing. Who would have thought that you would be sitting in front of me now, asking me to get back together with you. Making your promises...telling me that you have changed. Well Dennis, I don't believe you have changed at all. I can tell by the way you are talking right now. Please, just go. It's never going to work between us. I'm happy now. There was a time that I loved you more than I loved myself. When you broke up with me, you actually did me a favor. I finally learned to love myself. Please go. There really is nothing more to say. Just leave, OK?

*Notes:*_____

_____

_____

Life Goes On
Drama
40+

She has watched her daughter go through a tragic experience, and picking up the pieces is not so easy. These are a mother's words of encouragement.

Easy? I know this hasn't been easy. Nobody said it was going to be easy. But it has been four months since he died, and you are still sleeping your days away. I hate to see you compromise your life like this, Baby. Look around you. You have a beautiful daughter who loves you very much. You are surrounded by family and friends, by people who love and care about you. Doesn't any of that matter? Or has your whole existence been based on your love for Philip? Accept it, Honey. He's gone. He is never coming back. But you are still here, and you're alive. You must go on. Death is a part of life. Yes, it's painful, but don't make it debilitating. You're still young, and you have your whole life ahead of you. Try to be thankful for the time you did have with him. He will always be right here, in your heart. Come on, get out of bed and go take a shower. I'll take you shopping. It's going to be OK. Just give it some time.

Notes:_____

_____

Dual Deception
Drama
20+

After coming home late, she finds herself being questioned by her hypocritical husband.

Where was I? I was at Shelly's house. Well, it got late, and my batteries in my mobile ran out. What's the problem here? Why are you questioning me so much? So, I didn't call. What's the big deal? Get off my case, Martin! You were worried? Is that so? Give me a break! Do you know how many times I have sat up at night waiting for you, wondering where you were? I used to call everybody we knew looking for you. Just to let you know, your buddy, Dave, is your worst alibi of all. Oh, and your line, "Oh, Babe, I have to work late tonight," has gotten a little old. I'm not stupid! Why are you so concerned about me anyway? You are never this concerned about where I am. Between mistresses, are we? Or is it *do as I say and not as I do*? I have been wanting to say this for a really long time. I'm done. We're over.

Notes:_____

_____

_____

I'm Not a Junky
Drama
18+

A drug addict sends her boyfriend out to purchase a quick fix only to find out that he is as much of a junky as she is.

Took you long enough. Baby, where's the stuff? Come on. Where's my stuff, Baby? Give it to me. What do you mean you did it all? All of it? You only had to go two miles, and you already did it all? I gave you the money to get it for me, dammit! We were going to do it together. Don't you dare call me a junky. I am not the junky here. You do the candy as much as I do. A pro? Yeah, thanks to you, I've learned to be a pro from a pro. I can shoot up in less than 30 seconds and not miss a beat. Man, I knew I shouldn't have trusted you. When will I learn to listen to myself? Get out! Get out of my house, now! You're no good for me anyway. I hate my life. I hate the way I feel, and I hate you! What a waste. I can do better than you anyway. You are such a loser. Yeah, you're the junky, not me. Get out! Get out!

Notes:_____

_____

_____

I Miss You
Drama
18+

When she looks down at her own hands, she is reminded of her.

When I look at my hands, I remember that my grandmother and I have the exact same hands. Soft, long delicate fingers with small nails that never seem to grow. When I look around my house, I see what was hers, that over the years, she gave me. Pictures, a typewriter, dishes. When I think about it, she has been one of the strongest women I have known. She was so dignified. Kind of like Jackie O. She endured so much pain in her life and yet she never let the worst get the best of her. She was the one who kept the family together. She always gave love and support, no matter what. Yeah, I miss her…even though she sits right in front of me, staring… trying to figure out who I am. That's when I take her hand and tell her that I am somebody who loves her very much. You see, my grandmother is still alive, but she has gone somewhere else. I would like to think she is in a happy place, feeling young and free. Even though she sits right in front of me.

Notes:_____

_____

_____

Living Scared
Drama
20+

Life has become more complicated. Domestic violence has become her own reality.

We were together for six months before he actually hit me the first time. Usually it was just a shove here and there. Then one night we were at a restaurant, and he saw this guy looking over at me. When we got home, all of the sudden I found myself pinned down on the kitchen floor with a fist headed right for my face. He said it was my fault that the guy was looking at me and how dare I dress the way I did. I never even saw the guy. That night I was scared to death. My face was black and blue and completely swollen. I couldn't leave the house for days. The next morning, I woke up to a huge vase full of flowers by my bed. He said he was sorry for what he did. And he truly was sorry. I have endured that kind of treatment for two years now. He is always sorry. I can't take it anymore. I know I need to leave him, but he has gotten so obsessed. He says he can't live without me. If I leave him now, I'm afraid he may try to kill me. I don't know what to do.

Notes:_____

_____

The Angel
Drama
18+

She has been in the hospital fighting a fatal illness. During the night, she is given an extraordinary gift. The next day, she describes the experience to her closest friend.

An angel came to me last night. It was so beautiful... nothing like I have ever seen before. Funny, I didn't wake up to a noise...I just woke up. All of the sudden my whole room began to light up. But it wasn't a bright light. It was more of a blue glow. Caroline, it was so amazing. For the first time in a long time, I felt a peace, and at that very moment, all of my pain was gone. Can you imagine? No pain from the medication, the chemo...none of it. I felt so alive. The angel showed me something. I am not afraid anymore. I know this sounds crazy, but the angel told me where I'm going to go, and to not be afraid anymore. I have been so afraid of dying, not knowing what is on the other side. Now, I know. And now, I'm not afraid anymore. None of us really ever know where we go after we die. Last night, I think I was given a grand tour.

Notes:_____

_____

_____

Hi Honey, I'm Home
Drama
20+

A miracle has taken place, yet her husband is not as enthusiastic about sharing the joy. Actually, he is feeling an exorbitant amount of fear at the moment.

Hi, Honey. How was your day? Good. Now come over here and sit down. I made a very special dinner tonight. We are going to celebrate. Well, I have something to tell you, Sweetheart. OK, deep breath...I'm, I'm pregnant. I am going to have your baby! I know this might come as a little bit of a shock, but...well, it must be fate. Come on, isn't it wonderful? Aren't you thrilled? What's wrong? What? Why do I get the feeling you are not very happy about this? Too soon? What do you mean? We have been married for three years. How long were you planning on waiting? And when did it become your decision? What happened to "us"? When we got married, you never said you didn't want children. You never said a word. Look, I want to be a mother so bad I can taste it. Come on, what else is there? A child will bring us closer together, not pull us apart. The day this baby is born, you will be the happiest man on this earth. You'll see. I promise.

Notes:_____

_____

_____

Passing Strangers
Drama
18+

Before the bus heads out, she walks across the street to get something to eat. She makes conversation with the woman who is standing in line at the hotdog stand.

What does it say on that menu up there? I can't read that up there. Three bucks for a combo meal, huh? I guess that's cheaper than if I buy the hot dog, chips and drink separately. That's what I was gonna order. Yeah, look at that. It's a whole dollar cheaper. I've gotta save my money as much as I can. I have a two day bus trip back to Nebraska. Las Vegas just hasn't been an easy place to make a start. Spent a little too much time on my back, if you know what I mean. Plus, everybody is out to get ya around here. I have lots of friends back home. Lots of family too. Yeah, mustard and cheese, no ketchup, huh? Not too much cheese neither. The engine in my car blew up last week and that's when I decided to move back. Yeah, it's time to go back. I gave it a good five-month try though. Well, hey, see ya. Gotta go catch my bus.

Notes:_____

_____

_____

Am I a Good Parent?
Drama
30+

A mother of a teenager realizes deep down that her daughter is in trouble. The answers seem out of reach. After all, this can't be happening to her family.

At this point, I don't know what to do. She spends all of her time in her room. She hasn't eaten dinner with us in weeks. She is just not herself anymore. I feel so distant from her. When she looks at me, I feel like an alien. But when her friends call, she spends hours talking to them. Is this the way teenagers normally act, or do I have a problem here? Erica seems too far away. I'm worried about her. At night I lay awake wondering about the mistakes I have made. Have I been a good mother? Have I always been there for my child? Maybe all of my fears have become reality. Is she hanging out with the wrong crowd? Could she be doing drugs? What I *do* know is that she has stopped communicating with me. I'm losing my baby. I feel so helpless; and yet I know I need to do something. But what? What am I supposed to do?

Notes:_____
_____
_____

Unfinished Business
Drama
18+

He called her on the phone and informed her of his choice not to live anymore. Now, his pain would become her reality.

I never realized that you hurt so badly. Thanks a lot. Now, I hurt too. Except, my heart won't stop hurting. I miss you so much and I miss what we will never have. What was so bad to make you want to leave? I don't get it. You had so much going for you. And what about us? You ended us, just like that. You told me that you loved me, then you said goodbye, all in the same breath. They all keep telling me that you were selfish and screwed up, that I should be angry. The bottom line is, they are angry at you for my pain. They say that suicide is the ultimate selfish act. Maybe so, but friends are supposed to be there for each other, especially in a time of need, aren't they? And you needed me. You said you needed me. But now what? I live with this guilt and this pain and I can't seem to shake it. I should have believed you when you said you were going to do it...but I didn't. Oh...this is crazy. Look at me. I'm talking to a piece of concrete...as if he is here...sitting in front of me, listening.

Notes:_____

_____

Murder to What Degree?
Drama
18+

After a life of abuse from her father, she begins to justify killing him to a police psychologist..

Angry? Anger was just part of it. I grew up with the nice house and the nice cars. I even had my own credit cards. I guess you could say I had everything. That's what my friends thought anyway. But...I also had my Dad. Everyday. Maybe it was his work that got to him. I don't know. What I do know is that the only time my dad showed me love...was after he beat me. Oh yeah. He would come home drunk, bouncing off the walls. He had this rage inside of him. He always had a crazy look in his eyes when he was drunk. He would shove me around, yelling at me...telling me that everything was always my fault. And he'd get this close to my face. He loved that, because when he was close, he could see my fear. My whole body would shake. Yeah, he loved that. I can still smell him. I'm lucky that hair grows back. Do you know how much it hurts to have your hair pulled out of your head by the handfuls? Yeah, I hated him, every single day. Put yourself in my shoes. Wouldn't you have shot him too?

Notes:_____

_____

_____

Out of the Closet
Drama
20+

Falling in love has never felt so good. Without much thought of what the reaction may be, she tells her mother about the person she loves.

Actually, I am doing fantastic. For the first time in my life I am really happy. Mom, I have fallen in love! Ah... no...no...you haven't met him...because *he* is not a *him*. Well, he is a she. Now don't look at me like that. Why don't you show me the rule book that says you can only fall in love with the opposite sex. Her name is Angie, and she makes me happy. Truly happy. That's what should matter here. When I talk, she listens...and I find that I want to listen to her. She makes me laugh. I feel like I have no worries when I am with her. Our relationship is so uncomplicated. I can breathe. Mom, I have never experienced this with any of the men in my life. Tell me, can you think of a better description of what love is? I'm happy and that's all that should matter, right? Mom? Ok, I'm going to say this once. I don't need your approval, but I sure would love your support. Please look at me. Mom?

*Notes:*_____

_____

Goodbye
Drama
30+

The cancer has taken over. Her time is short. Bedridden and breathless, she tries to be strong for her daughter.

Come over here, Honey, and sit down next to me. Hey, hey, hey, no tears. Do you realize that I love you more than anything in this world? You have been my happiness, my joy, my everything. I thank you so much for that. You have made my life so complete. Listen to me. Let me ask you a question. Do you think that after I'm gone, any of that will change? Absolutely not. I am going to be watching you every minute. Maybe more than you will want me to. Just because my physical body is dying, doesn't mean that I am. All of this is just temporary...just skin and organs. But I'm inside. I am going to live forever and so will you. Try to remember that. The cancer is just a way of changing direction in my life, that's all. I know that makes you angry, but think about it. Please, Baby, you are going to be OK. I will always be with you, because I love you. Don't you see? You are my daughter and that will keep us together forever. I know, I know. I'm going to miss you too, Sweetheart.

Notes:_____

_____

_____

The Good Ole Days
Drama
60+

Watching her granddaughter get ready for a date triggers fond memories of her past.

I sure miss those days. Life was full of romance. The music was soft and all about love. I remember those hot summer days when we would sip on freshly squeezed lemonade and socialize with the closest of friends. Dating in my day was so different than it is now. If you had a gentleman caller, he first needed to pursue the permission of your father before he could see you on a regular basis. My dates usually consisted of a visit in our sitting parlor or going to the ice cream shop down the street for a cherry soda. Watching you get ready for your date brings back so many memories. Are you nervous? I guess the feeling of butterflies never go away. That was how I felt every time your grandfather came to pick me up. Life was so simple then, yet so wonderful. Full of romance it was. Well, Dear, you just look beautiful. Promise me, you won't come home too late, OK?

Notes:_____

_____

_____

Speaking From Experience
Drama
30+

It is human nature to become the product of our environment. Guest speaker, Ellen Welch, gives her speech during a motivational seminar. She is the perfect example of someone who decided to go against the grain.

First, I would like to take this time to introduce myself. My name is Ellen Welch. I own and operate one of the largest computer software companies is the United States. I was born in a small mid-western town with a population of about 300. My family was in the farming business. That meant that we all helped out with feeding the animals, hoeing the crops, those sort of things. Not one of my family members attended college and only half completed high school. At the age of sixteen, I made a conscious decision. I would not live out my life in a small town as a farm girl. At the age of eighteen, I took that first step and gave myself the opportunity to become educated. Once I finally realized what I enjoyed doing, I continued to take a proactive posture in every decision I made. To me, success covers a wide spectrum, personally and professionally. You create your own way. Give yourself the opportunity to be successful. It is all up to you, because nobody is going to do it for you. Thank you.

Notes:_____

_____

_____

Support
Drama
20+

The coach of a girl's basketball team gives understanding and support to one of the team members who is having second thoughts about staying on the team.

Jenny, come on over here. I want to talk to you for a minute. I have been hearing a little talk from some of the girls that you are thinking of quitting the team. Is that right? I know that this sport has been a challenge for you, but, hey, the challenge is what it is all about. I don't want to see you quit and miss an experience that can give you so much. So what if you don't win every game. This is not about winning. It's all about playing and giving all you've got. Don't ever forget the fact that you have something to offer, something different, something special. That's the way it will be for the rest of your life. Who cares if it is not right for everybody else. As long as it is right for you. Listen, I want you to know we appreciate your participation on this team. You are a big part of it. Think about it, OK?

Notes:_____

_____

The Presentation
Drama
25+

Her career is based on the corporate world of technology. As potential customers flock around the booth, she begins her presentation.

Hello Sir. Please have a seat and I will begin the presentation. Great. Looks like everyone has taken a seat. Welcome to Technology 2040. We are proud to bring you the latest in today's technology. How many of you own a computer? Technology 2040 has developed the most secured system today to handle all of your needs. Let's face it, ladies and gentlemen, our world is changing and the year 2000 not only represented, but also instigated change. We have come a long way from black and white television and eight track cassettes. Yes, remember those? Rotary telephones, think about it. Remember, at the time we sent the first men up in space, all mathematical calculations were done by hand. How quick can you divide 78,249 by 3,529 and then multiply by 74. We have progressed to the age of plasma television, digital communication, the internet, and yes, wireless personal computers. Today's technology is growing faster than society can keep up. Come with me now on a journey through the next 40 years. Would any of you like to take a guess of where we will be then?

Notes:_____

_____

_____

The Loss of a Friend
Drama
30+

Her husband has seemingly entered some sort of middle age crisis and has emotionally strayed away from the marriage. She takes a stand and makes one more attempt to reach him, for she truly loves him.

Stop it! Just stop it! Don't you ever talk to me like that again. Quit acting as if you are the only person in this world that matters. I matter too, you know. Or have you forgotten that? I have committed every ounce of energy I have to this marriage. I have given you my best years! Not to mention all of the support, upholding your corporate image, the children. There was a time when I saw you as loving, giving and supportive. You were my best friend. Now, I see you as self-loving, self-giving and self-centered. What has happened to you? I want you back. I want the man I married back. Please, Sean, just talk to me.

Notes:_____

_____

_____

The Pain
Drama
30+

She finally musters up her courage to speak up in a Survivors of Suicide support group. As she shares her experience regarding her daughter, she begins to regret sharing her feelings altogether.

Hi, my name is Tessa Rhodes, and I am a survivor of suicide. I have been coming to this support group for five weeks now and I haven't said a word. I just sit here listening to your stories and sharing your pain. (She clears her throat) Uh, where do I start? My daughter committed suicide four months ago. They found her in her car, parked behind a shopping mall, with a gun lying on the passenger seat. I just can't accept that my baby was feeling that much pain to take her own life. Growing up, she was such a vibrant child. Full of life. I had no idea she was so unhappy. I thought I knew my daughter. I thought she would come to me if she needed help. I guess I was the person who was the furthest away from her. I should have been there for her. See...I knew I would start crying. What good is it to talk about it anyway? Why relive this pain over and over and over again?

Notes:_____

_____

Desperation
Drama
18+

A woman witnesses a horrible traffic accident that has just occurred on a rural highway far from city limits. She is hysterical during the time that the first officer arrives on the scene.

Yes Officer, I saw the whole thing. Those people are really hurt in that car over there. There is blood everywhere. No, I haven't been drinking. Yes, I did. I saw the whole thing. That cement truck over there just never stopped. The light was red, too. It ran right into that green car. Then the blazer hit the truck. They tried to stop, but it was too late. It was awful. What? Wait here? Oh, no Sir, I don't want to just wait here. The people in that car need help. I have a blanket in my trunk. Can I go get the blanket? Yes, I know the ambulance is on it's way, but they could be awhile. Please, Sir, I can hear a baby crying. What good is it for me to stay here! Why won't you let me help? Please, let me help that baby!

Notes:_____

_____

_____

Unconditional Love
Drama
40 +

A mother learns of her son's sexuality and overcomes the shock. In the end, she gives what any mother would, unconditional love.

Please...please, Honey, wait a minute. Let me explain why your father and I reacted the way we did. As you can imagine, shock was our first reaction. Disbelief came in as a close second. We have been so proud of you and your successes and we couldn't understand why you didn't have a young lady in your life. Listen, when you have children of your own, you have certain ideas of how they will grow up. You tend to think about what kind of careers they may choose...what interesting places they will travel to...and even at what point in their lives will they get married. Please understand, Honey, I have even fantasized about how many grandchildren there will be running around this house. Maybe it is unfair to have expectations of your children, but that's what mothers do. I never thought that my son would be gay. It never entered my mind. But you know what? You are my son and I love you very much...no matter what. Give your father some time. He'll come around.

Notes:_____

_____

Wasted Time
Drama
25+

She tells a friend about her relationship with her boyfriend. The more she talks, the more she realizes that she is involved in a dead end.

I don't know why I've wasted three years with him. From the beginning he said he was in no rush to get married. No rush? I'd say! It's obvious. He's afraid of commitment. What made me think I could change his mind? What made me think he was worth it? Who knows? He's the type of man who thinks sitting in front of the T.V. together is quality time. But that's all he always wants to do. I guess because that involves the least amount of effort. Now that I think about it, he's pretty much of a slob. I pick up after him constantly. And we never talk. Why is that? When we were dating, he was "Mr. Conversationalist." Now, I'm lucky to get a small laugh out of him. He has changed so much. It makes me wonder. Is it him? Would he be the same way with another woman? Or is it me? It just seems like I have completely carried the relationship and he has taken it all for granted.

Notes:_____

_____

_____

The News
Drama
18+

They inform her of her father's unexpected death. As she starts to process the realization, she tells her friend how she is feeling.

How do I feel? To be honest, I don't know how I'm supposed to feel right now. You know, I didn't even ask how he died? Part of me wants to cry and part of me says good riddance. I remember when I was 7 years old, he took me to the zoo, just the two of us. I will never forget that day, because on that day, he was just my dad. He bought me cotton candy, and he even let me ride the elephant by myself. On that day I felt only love for him. As I grew older, I started to remember the nights that he would come into my room...and I could smell his drunken breath. That's when I hated him. My skin would crawl. I learned to go somewhere else. I had this elevator that I would climb into, and it would take me directly into space to cruise through the stars. In my mind, I was as far away from him as possible. Now, he is dead. Why is it that I have this urge to honor him? He put me through so much hurt and yet, I loved him so much.

Notes:_____

_____

_____

The Ultimate Betrayal
Drama
25+

Her husband's guilt prevails. After she learns the truth, she confronts her friend.

What's wrong? What's wrong? What do you think is wrong? How could you let me go this long not knowing that you slept with him? Excuse me but I think that is pertinent information considering I am married to the man and you are my so-called "best friend." Don't...don't even try to explain. If you think about it, there is really absolutely nothing to explain. To me, it's very simple. I leave town on business for a few days and you two decide to get lonely together. How damn convenient! At this point, I don't know what I am going to do. I am in shock. My head is literally spinning right now. The two people who are closest to me just screwed me in the worst way possible. It never occurred to me that either one of you would cross that line. My God, if you can't trust your husband and your best friend, who can you trust?

Notes:_____

_____

Things To Do
Drama
25+

As she goes through life, her "To Do List" becomes much more complex.

As I sat at my desk, my attention was drawn to a pile of miscellaneous notes and messages. The pile consisted of different colored post-it notes, along with torn pages that I had been avoiding for weeks. I began to go through it, and one note caught my attention immediately. I guess, because it had an immediate message. Strategically placed on a yellow post-it note, in my own hand writing, were the words...Things To Do. Number one: milk, eggs, bread. Two: mail credit card bill. Three: overcome my depression. And at that very moment my whole body became tense. I was reminded of how unhappy I have been. I realized that even though I could still go to the grocery store or to the post office, I was unhappy, even sad. Or more appropriately put...depressed. Whatever happened to the simple reminder notes like, "take out the trash" or "pick up the dry cleaning" or "dinner with Steve on Friday." But this message is very overwhelming...beyond belief. Milk, eggs and dry cleaning are easy, but the depression. If I could overcome it, I would. If I could feel better, I would. The words are simple, yet the message seems impossible.

Notes:_____

_____

_____

Close to You
Drama
18+

As she listens to a Sinatra song with her grandfather, she realizes the passion he had for her grandmother.

Even though he is in his eighties, his passion runs strong and he insists on playing his favorite song for me. He sits in his comfortable chair with his head tilted down, waiting for the very first note to grab his heart. As I watch him listen, there is no question that he feels every word, and hears every tempo, in every instrument. Then, I find myself in his world. And I too feel the romance, love, and his passion. I wonder, who is he thinking about? I don't dare ask him. I can only imagine who holds his heart during this song. At the moment, he is truly in love. He is completely connected with "her," whomever she is. But to me it is clear. She is beautiful and sincere. She is loving, giving and true. Yes, it is her. How could it be anyone else? She is the one he is thinking of. Of course, he longs for her...as it should be. Yes, I remember her the same way.

Notes:_____

_____

Denial
Drama
20+

Her family has just committed her into a drug and alcohol rehab center. She now faces her first group therapy session and tries to justify why she doesn't belong.

Maxine...Maxine Fairbanks, the woman of many secrets and lovers, you know, from the soap, *Coral Reef.* You people don't know anything, do you? Look at you all. Let me tell you the way I see it. I look around this room at a bunch of losers who have never even lived life. Just look at you and look at me. It is obvious that your idea of going out to dinner is going to the closest buffet restaurant. Yet, I have a personal Chef, Jon. Look, I am an actress, a true performer. I make people like you...feel. Dr. Watts, I don't mean to be disrespectful, but it is clear that I am here by mistake. It seems that I have a few paranoid family members who think I need help. But I am not like these people. They are the ones with the problems, not me. I have maids. I go to work everyday in a limousine. I am somebody! I am Maxine Fairbanks, the woman of many secrets and lovers. I am not a drug addict. It's just for fun. I'm not hooked. This is all just a huge misunderstanding. I'd like to use the phone please. Why are you all just sitting there staring at me. I said that I would like to use the phone...now! I said now!

Notes:_____

_____

_____

Comedy

Staying Single
Comedy
20+

After trying a few live-in boyfriends, she decides that living single is the way to go.

I am in no rush to get married or to move in with someone. I've tried that *living together stuff.* No thank you. The minute he puts his clothes in your dirty clothes hamper, you become, *maid.* During my last boyfriend, I decided to go on strike and I stopped doing his laundry, altogether. He finally caught on after about four days of picking his dirty shirts up off the closet floor and smelling the arm pits. He would actually look at me in a very confused state and say, "Hey, if it looks clean." Fortunately, I never had to witness his decision process on which dirty pair of underwear he picked for the day. But I still had the visual, and at that point I knew where that particular relationship was headed. I think I'll stay single and live alone for a while. As far as my date's laundry habits are concerned, well, what I don't know won't hurt me.

Notes:_____

_____

_____

Secrets
Comedy
20+

She may feel that keeping a secret is one of her personal strengths. However, gossip is her biggest weakness. These days whom can you trust?

They say women can't keep a secret. I have never understood that. I am a woman and I happen to be the most loyal friend anyone could ever have. Ask my best friend Lois. My lips are sealed forever. I promise. OK, I'll prove it to you. Did I ever mention a word about Larry Murphy getting fired from his job because he got caught, you know...in his office? He claimed his wife had been getting a lot of headaches lately. Or, did I ever repeat that Lois saw Ms. Jenkins and Mr. Tanner swapping spit behind the church, during service? Did you ever hear that story? Huh? Well, see? I never said a word. Have you heard this one? Mary Sue sneaks out every Wednesday night to meet George Ferrell. Believe me, they aren't just talkin' town politics. Handcuff me to a ceiling fan and turn it on full blast. Beat me if you have to. I'll never tell...that Lois hides a Playgirl underneath her mattress. Shhhhhh. Don't tell anybody. Being my best friend and all, she would kill me if she found out I said a word.

Notes:_____

_____

Sports Fanatic
Comedy
20+

She now must face the harsh reality of losing her husband to football.

What is it with men and sports? You know what I'm talking about. You say something to him, but there is no response because he is glued to the TV. That is proof right there that men have an incredible ability to focus. But there's just one problem. Focus seems to peak at game time instead of dinner time. The bottom line is, my husband has become more interested in football than me. When we were dating, the words *tight end* referred to my tight end. Now that we are married, he is more interested in the tight end on the San Francisco 49er's. Last week I put on my sexiest lingerie. As I strolled in front of the TV he said to me, "Nice babe, later huh?" Little does he know, the only kind of penetration he will be experiencing is by the guys from the 49er's. I have to face it. My husband is gone. There is no hope. The only light I see at the end of the tunnel is a big screen TV and more chips and dip. Great. Should I plan his funeral now or should I wait until football season ends?

Notes:_____

_____

The Price
Comedy
25+

Sometimes, giving a spouse too much control over finances can lead to problems. She found out the hard way.

Peter and I had been married for four years. We were actually married here in Las Vegas at the chapel on Main Street. Elvis attended our wedding. Well, not really, but you know what I mean. From then on, I always let Peter take care of our finances. All I cared about was that I had extra money for shopping. Then one day I realized that we had a big problem. Big Benny Mahoney came knocking on our door. He said that my Peter better come up with five thousand dollars or he would garnish his spaghetti with my Peter's toes. I tried to use my wit and good charm, but you know what Big Benny said to me? That he could get any girl he wanted and why would he waste his time on a washed up broad like me. Can you believe he said that? For the past year I have been here working as a waitress to pay off Peter's debt. As soon as I'm done paying off Big Benny, I am going to earn enough money to divorce Peter, if I ever find him. Boy, was he a mistake! Big mistake!

Notes:_____

_____

_____

Infatuation
Comedy
18+

Be careful what you ask for. You just might get it.

I had been watching him forever. I'd watch him at the gym and basically...drool. Everyone tried to tell me that he wasn't that great. All I knew was that he had a great "you know what." He was to die for. Well, of course the minute he met me, he asked me out. It all started that night when he asked me to dance. I started to groove and, well, he started to move. "Thankful" wasn't the word when that song ended. So I suggested we go get something to eat...anything to get off the dance floor. I do have a reputation to uphold, you know. I guess it was the cherry tomato that did it. I knew the minute he stuck it in his mouth. Do you know how difficult it is to clean little tomato seeds out of your ear? Very. Anyway, I dumped him. So hey, know any single guys?

Notes:_____

_____

Reality Check
Comedy
25+

Being a woman is not as easy as it seems. After experiencing the demands of being a wife, she can finally empathize with her mother's life.

Come on ladies. The dreams we had as little girls are just plain overrated. Think about it. As little girls, somewhere along the line we got this idea that when we grew up, we would meet a perfect man...who would love us...and only us. Yes, that excluded any other little girls. We would have two children, he would take care of us and of course, we'd live happily ever after. Reality check! Over 50% of the marriages in this country end up in divorce. Prince Charming is out of shape by the age of forty, you work fifty hours a week, raise the rug rats, become Martha Stewart during meal time and if that's not enough, you are expected to play the lead role in *Babes in Babesland* for your husband...all night. Yes, all night, because some pill called Viagra just came out on the market and Mr. Charming just had to get himself some. No wonder we dream as little girls. Reality sounds exhausting! Who wants to dream about that?

Notes:_____

_____

_____

Dating Again
Comedy
18+

Feeling slightly helpless, she watches her mother enter the dating world. Maybe mom isn't thinking clearly. At this point, she must put it into fate's hands.

It has been absolutely crazy since my mom decided to start dating again. She goes out almost every night...and not always with the same guy. She says she needs to be "open to what is out there." I say, "Hey, if he's cute, go for it." My mom signed up with a dating service. She asked me if I thought she was being desperate. I said, "Of course not," nodding my head yes. As if I'm going to tell her the truth. You should see some of these guys. First of all, my mom thinks she has an age range of about fifteen years. I have seen everything from Mr. College Grad to Mr. Executive. I think her worst looking date was Stan. He stood no taller than five feet, and his nose was almost as tall as he was. One night as my mom was leaving, I said, "Hey Mom, you may need a booster chair for this one." She didn't find that very funny. The worst part is that she likes Stan. The next time he came to pick her up, he was wearing platform shoes. I guess he heard me. Oops!

Notes:_____

_____

Forget Love
Comedy
25+

After a bad experience, she decides that love is not the answer. She explains to a friend that settling for "comfortable" is what she wants.

Listen honey, I won't even date a man unless he makes six figures. Anything less is a complete waste of my time. I prefer to live a certain lifestyle, a way that is, well, you know, comfortable. I want to belong to the most elite country club, take tennis lessons from the most adorable tennis pro, and yes, I want my own personal masseuse. There are plenty of men out there who can give me that. All you have to do is look at the shoes. You can always tell how much a man makes by his shoes, Darling. Love? Oh, please. Love is the furthest thing from my mind. I fell in love once, then fell right out of it when I walked in on him, in his office, with his secretary. Should I say, she was taking way too many notes. No, no, no. Falling in love is so overrated. Really, there is so much more to life than that. Besides, I get more love from my dog, Hercules. He could care less about how I look before my makeup, and well, he does everything I tell him to do.

Notes:_____

_____

_____

Men Do the Funniest Things
Comedy
20+

The observations of a single female.

Going through life as an attractive single woman can be very entertaining. Men do the funniest things. I should buy airtime and educate these poor guys. For example; you're waiting in your car at a stoplight. I don't know about you but I can feel it when some suitor is looking my way. I haven't yet, but boy am I tempted to stick my finger right up my nose to search for the big one. And may I remind all of you men out there, I don't recall my eyes being located on my chest. When a man stares at my chest, I want to say, "Get your own bags!" Then again, if you think about it…if men had breasts…uh, never mind. I'll pass on that visual. And what is it about their motorcycles, or more appropriately, their *rides*? The last time I was taken for a *ride*, I ended up with a face full of spit going fifty miles an hour. No thank you. Hey, and shame on all of you married men who get a slight case of whiplash just to get a glimpse of me as I walk by. I hope your neck hurts. Finally, get rid of all of those gold chains. You look like you have just invested in a *rapper's starting kit.*

Notes:_____

_____

Opportunity Lost
Comedy
20+

In this case, a little too much game playing may have resulted in an opportunity lost.

Guess what? He finally called! Four days later, but he called. You know me, I've been pacing the floor just waiting for his call. No, I didn't answer it. I let the machine pick it up, Silly. He left a message saying how much fun he had on our date and he asked that I call him back. Well sure that's a good sign. We both had a great time. You know, Mel, he is the first guy that I have really hit it off with in a long time. Plus he is absolutely gorgeous, not to mention successful. No, I haven't called back yet. Please! I don't want to come off desperate. It took him four days to call me, I think I will make him wait at least seven. Oh really, Mel, you just don't know how to play the game, do you? Oh stop! That is not how I blew it with Ryan. He doesn't call me back because his secretary swears he's out of town on business. Of course I believe that. Why would she lie? Oh, calm down, will you? I know what I'm doing.

Notes:_____

_____

Promises, Promises, Promises
Comedy
20+

Who says money doesn't change people? As she excitedly informs Clara that she won the lottery, in the same breath, she promises that the money won't change her.

You are not going to believe this! I won the lottery! One hundred thousand dollars! Yes! Me! I can't believe it either. I have never won anything in my life. Now Clara, I promise you right here and right now that I will not let the money change me. We will always be friends, OK? I am so excited! I can't believe it! I have to go down to the lottery office tomorrow to pick up my check. The press will be there and everything. Oh, what do you think I should wear? I'm going to be in the public eye, you know. Hey, maybe I should get a boob job. I used to thank God for this miserable body he gave me. Who was I kidding? Now I can afford it! Besides, when Sabrina Fairfield walks into the office with her boobs pushed up to her chin, I would like to push my boobs up right back at her. Actually, maybe a little tuck here and there wouldn't hurt either. Oh, don't worry Clara. I told you, I won't let the money change me...just a few of my imperfections. Loosen up will ya?

Notes:_____

_____

_____

What You Don't Know Won't Hurt You
Comedy
30+

This devoted housewife is no dummy. When her husband steps out of line, he pays the consequences, sometimes without even knowing it.

Lately, Jerry has been getting on my nerves. If he leaves that toilet lid up one more time I'm gonna...I'm gonna add a tablespoon of cat food to his meatloaf. Jerry never likes to hear me complain. He says I nag. I hear it over and over and over, "Why can't you just be quiet and stay in the kitchen?" So I've learned to release my frustrations in other ways. When Jerry asks me to make him hot chocolate, I smile and say, "sure Darling," and I head right for Banister's doggy bowl. No fresh bottled water for Jerry? Not for my Jerry. One time Jerry got me so mad, I hid a rotten egg in his office and sewed a whoopee cushion to his office chair. He went through three different secretaries that week. Poor Jerry. I wish he would learn, because my next batch of brownies may be full of Ex-lax.

Notes:_____

_____

_____

Holding Out
Comedy
18+

Her friend pokes fun at her for being a hopeless romantic.

I know you think I am a hopeless romantic. You go right ahead and waste your time on every Mr. Never. But there is someone out there for me, and I am going to hold out for him. He is out there, and he too is hoping that he will meet me soon. Trust me. It will happen. Just you wait, one day I will turn the corner, and there he will be. I won't even hesitate when I see him. I will know, in my heart. And your point is? OK, so if he ends up being the bag-boy at the corner grocery or a street cleaner, then so be it. But I don't think my soul mate would be a... Go ahead, keep laughing. Your soul mate will probably end up being a gorilla.

Notes:_____

_____

_____

Notes:

Notes:

Notes:

Notes:

Notes:

Notes:

Notes:_____

Notes:_____
_____
_____
_____
_____
_____
_____
_____
_____
_____
_____
_____
_____
_____
_____
_____
_____
_____
_____
_____
_____
_____
_____
_____
_____
_____
_____
_____

Coming Soon...

Monólogos para Actores: Temas Poderosos para Niños y Adolescentes

To Order

Audition Monologues: Power Pieces for Women

$14.95

Add $3.00 for Shipping and Handling

Add $.50 for each additional book

To order through the **internet**: www.auditionmonologues.com

To order through the **mail**, send check, money order or credit card # and expiration date along with the following order form to:

Lucid Solutions

P.O. Box 32141

Mesa, Arizona 85275-2141

- -

Audition Monologues: Power Pieces for Women

How many? _____ (Qty) X $14.95/ea................ = _____

Sales Tax (For Arizona residents only, add 7.8%)..... = _____

Shipping/Handling ....= _____

($3.00 for first book, $0.50/each additional book)

Total = _____

Check#:_____ MC:_____ Visa:_____ AMEX:_____

Discover:_____ Money Order #:_____

Credit Card #:_____-_____-_____-_____

Expiration Date:_____/_____/_____

Card Member's Signature:

_____

I give permission to charge my card for the said order

Please print the following customer billing information:

Ship my order to:

Name:_____

Address:_____

City:_____ State:_____ Zip:_____

Phone Number:_____/_____/_____

Email Address:_____

Also available:

Audition Monologues: Power Pieces for Kids and Teens

About the Author...

Deborah Maddox has over fifteen years experience marketing and developing models and actors on an international level. Ms. Maddox continues to work as an Agent and currently resides in Arizona with her daughter.

Also by Deborah Maddox
"Audition Monologues: Power Pieces for Kids and Teens"

Coming soon...
"Monólogos para Actores: Temas Poderosos para Niños y Adolescentes"

I will never close another door
before I have opened it,

I will never not open a door
that stands before me,

Fear has lost it's power and
it will never prevail again,

I will live the experience,
not just dream about it.

Deborah Maddox

Printed in the United States
25952LVS00001B/139-213

9 780971 682719